Finding Myself

Joe Pignataro

Copyright © 2014 Joe Pignataro.

All rights reserved. No part of this book may be used or reproduced by any means, graphic, electronic, or mechanical, including photocopying, recording, taping or by any information storage retrieval system without the written permission of the publisher except in the case of brief quotations embodied in critical articles and reviews.

Inner Light Publishing books may be ordered through booksellers or by contacting:

Inner Light Publishing
www.innerlightpublish.com
innerlightpublishing@gmail.com

Because of the dynamic nature of the Internet, any web addresses or links contained in this book may have changed since publication and may no longer be valid. This is a work of non-fiction. The views expressed in this work are solely those of the author and do not necessarily reflect the views of the publisher and the publisher hereby disclaims any responsibility for them.

The author of this book does not dispense medical advice or prescribe the use of any technique as a form of treatment for physical, emotional, or medical problems without the advice of a physician, either directly or indirectly. The intent of the author is only to offer information of a general nature. In the event you use any of the information in this book for yourself, which is your constitutional right, the author and the publisher assume no responsibility for your actions.

ISBN: 978-0-9924628-5-7 (sc)
ISBN: 978-0-9924628-6-4 (e)

Table of Contents

Dedication..6

Tribute to Chris Lane.................................8

CHAPTER 1..1

CHAPTER 2..5

CHAPTER 3..13

CHAPTER 4..16

CHAPTER 5..20

CHAPTER 6..33

CHAPTER 7..38

CHAPTER 8..41

CHAPTER 9..45

CHAPTER 10 54

CHAPTER 11 58

CHAPTER 12 71

CHAPTER 13 73

About the Author...................................79

Finding Myself

Dedication

To my mother Lucy, father Joe and sister Lisa. Without them pushing me to break through my comfort zone none of this would've been possible and I don't know where I would be without them.

To my group of Kokoda trekkers.
I wasn't sure I would have been able to complete the journey, yet your love, support and positivity shone through and we smashed it!
Back Track Adventures, T20 2013, Team of Champions
Renea
Mark
Trace
Michelle
Ian
Mark
Chad
Peter
Frank
James
Zac
John

Thank You All
Love You xx

Tribute to Chris Lane

To my best friend Chris Lane: you taught me so many lessons throughout our short but spectacular journey together. Not a day goes by where you're not on my mind. Love You Bud.

CHAPTER 1

In the middle of October 2012, I had the world at my feet and at that stage of my life I felt contented and pretty complete with myself. I was 4 years into my dream job with SEN radio covering all sport in the sporting capital of the world, my home town – Melbourne. I hadn't seen my mate "Checkers" for quite some time. We'd known each other since the age of 5; however, work and university commitments had their own challenges and we no longer had school holidays to rely on for our catch up sessions. We did, however, come together on a Wednesday evening to catch up for a laugh, reminisce about the past and look towards the future.

Sitting in a cafe on that Wednesday night we got talking about what was our favourite time of year – Christmas. Checkers loves the festive season, probably more than anyone I have ever met. In the past few years he has headed over to the USA to embrace his ultimate dream which is the "White Christmas". To see someone chase their dream and watching them follow it through to the end is the greatest satisfaction. Then one night I got swept up by the thought of how amazing the atmosphere would be over there during that time and made the decision that I would experience it for myself later that year.

Together, we decided on a 2 week blitz that

included Christmas, my birthday (December 27), the ultimate night club party to bring in the New Year and finishing with a week of snowboarding in the Alps somewhere to wind down and relax after the hectic opening week that we would experience. It all sounded fantastic and I couldn't wait to get home to bed, wake up the next morning and tell my parents of the decision I had made. I had come to the conclusion that I was ready to experience America, supposedly the pinnacle of the world.

The next morning swang around; I awoke without that same enthusiasm and buzz I had the night before but still proceeded to tell my parents of my adventurous idea. As my parents had always have been, they were supportive of the idea. They encouraged me to go right ahead and do it if that was what I really wanted to do then. I've always been pushed by them to chase my wants, my needs and my dreams. I tend to take flight sometimes when I get swept up by emotion. This was definitely one of those occasions; I hadn't realised that just yet but it was only moments later that I came floating back down off cloud nine. I continued on with my day as usual before heading out to Flight Centre to get a quote for the ultimate trip.

Is it the job of people in travel to promote every single detail of every part of the world to prospective travellers? For some reason it's always positive and every part of the globe really is the "most amazing thing you'll ever see and you need to do it before you die!" Naturally, when I discussed my plans with my travel agent I got caught in the emotions and ticked off plans A, B, C, D all the way through to Z. Before I knew it I was at the end of the quote and set to sign a holiday that would cost around $10,000 (money that I didn't have). Something held me back from signing the bottom line and I chose to head home, speak to my parents, chat with my mate and sit quietly by myself trying to determine whether this really was the right decision and the best thing for me.

I have mentioned I have a job at SEN radio which I love and adore. I hadn't ever taken a holiday in the period I worked there and my body was desperate for one. Mentally I wasn't prepared to switch off and take that break; I didn't feel like I could voluntarily go and book a holiday to take time out, so when this opportunity came along to get to America I jumped at it.

In the quiet moments that afternoon I decided against going. I told Checkers of my decision and within an instant felt a shift of mood within me that told me America wasn't for me but a break from work definitely was.

I sat in silence with these thoughts for a little longer that afternoon before trying to let it go and going back to my day and letting life unfold in front of me. I kept getting this nagging feeling throughout the next couple of days to get back into this quiet moment. It was as if a voice was telling me to sit with this because the answer I was searching for wasn't far away from coming to me.

CHAPTER 2

Growing up in Melbourne and being mad about sports only means one thing around here. AFL. AFL footy is, according to us Melbournians, the greatest game in the world and we'll be damned if anyone tries to tell us otherwise. Promoting AFL is a battle within itself to anyone around Australia who sees otherwise and barracking for Collingwood is just as big a battle because anyone who doesn't follow the Magpie army hates them and in turn, when it comes to footy discussions, hates you!

There is an old saying when it comes to AFL; there are 2 types of supporters. The first are Collingwood supporters, the second are people who wish they had enough courage and guts to be one!

The reason for explaining my affiliation with the "Pies" and AFL is that every year since 1995 Collingwood takes on rivals Essendon on April 25 in what is now the game's traditional Anzac Day match, the biggest game of the year outside of the Grand Final with two of the biggest teams in the country. I've had the privilege of attending many of these games and each year it happened I learned a little bit more about Australia's war history and realized how lucky we all are these days because of our amazing war veterans from yesteryear.

Former coaches of both sides Mick Malthouse (Collingwood) and Kevin Sheedy (Essendon) were very big on emphasising that while at the end of the day it is just a game that they're out there playing, it is extremely important that the players who play in it and the supporters of the game have a greater understanding of the significance of playing a game on this day.

In this connection I was introduced to and taught about Kokoda. I was given a great understanding of what went on there many years back.

The **Kokoda Track campaign** *or* **Kokoda Trail campaign** *was part of the* Pacific War *of* World War II. *The campaign consisted of a series of battles fought between July and November 1942 between* Japanese *and* Allied—*primarily Australian*—*forces in what was then the Australian territory of* Papua. *Following a landing near Gona, on the north coast of* New Guinea, *on the night of 21/22 July, Japanese forces attempted to advance south over land through the mountains of the* Owen Stanley Range *to seize* Port Moresby *as part of a strategy of isolating Australia from the United States. Initially only limited Australian forces were available to oppose them, and after making rapid progress the Japanese* South Seas Force *under Major General* Tomitaro Horii *clashed with under strength Australian forces from the* Papuan Infantry Battalion *and the Australian* 39th Battalion *on 23 July at Awala, forcing them back to Kokoda. Following a confused night battle* *on 28/29 July, the Australians were again forced to withdraw. The Australians attempted to recapture Kokoda on 8 August without success which resulted in heavy casualties on both sides, and the 39th Battalion was subsequently forced back to Deniki. A number of Japanese attacks were subsequently fought off by the Australian* Militia *over the following week, yet by 14 August they began to withdraw over the Owen Stanley Range, down the* Kokoda Track *towards Isurava.*

During my final year of school in 2008, St Bernard's along with Victoria Police had organised for 10 boys to walk the Kokoda track; unfortunately it wasn't something that was offered to year 12's because of VCE exams and having to focus on our lives and careers once school was completed. From the moment I heard about trekking Kokoda I instantly fell in love with it. I immediately put it at the top of my "bucket list" ... At that stage the only other thing on my list was to see a Collingwood premiership (Which I was afforded the pleasure of in 2010). At that time I put the idea of walking the track on the back burner but never lost sight of the goal until the day I actually did it.

I never planned to go to university after school was over and always wanted to get into sport. I injured my knee in 2007. The doctors gave me my shattering news that I was never going to make it to the AFL. At 159cm I wasn't growing another millimetre; I knew that I was never going to make it to the top level anyway but it had never stopped me from trying to reach the top. As soon as the Docs confirmed that for me, I shifted my focus from trying to make it on the field to doing everything I could to make it off the field. I love my footy too much to let it pass me by and only be a fan of the game. So I set about putting plans in place to still reach the top level by combining my passions and hobbies.

My passion is obviously footy, but my hobbies include talking, and talking non-stop. So conversations with my mates became colourful and creative, using all sorts of descriptive words. I would turn just about everything into a piece of commentary. I strained my arm in my final 2 years of school by doing media studies, writing and producing radio pieces that would entertain and allow me to express myself creatively. I always battled a mental demon when playing footy as a teenager, because I wanted to be the best yet there were days when I never reached that "best" or the "zone" that I knew I could get to. Seeing someone who was fitter, taller and stronger, I lost my pre-game focus and fear took over which brought me crashing down and being very hard on myself. With radio though, I had a quiet confidence that I was good at radio, because of the looseness and creativeness that came with it. I'm driven to be the best I can be and the best in the business. Without any arrogance I can say that I'm confident in myself knowing I've put steps in place to succeed.

In 2009 my "big break" came when I got an opening into SEN radio in Melbourne, Australia's only 24 hours a day, 7 days a week talk back sports radio station. Being based in Melbourne means it is footy, footy, footy and in summer, cricket! That's about it in a nutshell. Between 2009 and August 17, 2013, I became a "yes man". So driven to succeed, I said yes to every opportunity thrown in my direction because I didn't want to miss out. I thought that I had to be there every time a position opened up; otherwise they would pick someone else for the spot and I would miss out. When the time came to pick between myself and another person for a position, I wanted the satisfaction of knowing that I'd be picked because of the hard yards I had put in previously. I began my career one morning a week on the breakfast program with Andrew Maher and Tim Watson, getting up at 4am to be home by 10am that morning. Not a bad lifestyle at all or so I thought, a lot of down time in the afternoon, plenty of time to catch up on other sports news, see friends and have a sleep.

It was great in the early days until the position became a daily job and SEN very quickly became my be all and end all so badly because I wanted it so much. I lost myself in my job throwing everything into it. In those moments I lost motivation for everything else. I made sacrifices that at the time I thought were the best thing for me, but I realise now they were unhealthy. They stunted my development and growth into other avenues of my life. By being so blindsided to succeed at work, I took away my greatest pleasure and outlet, which was playing footy on the weekends. In turn, that had a negative effect on my relationship with my greatest mentor and the first hero I ever had – my Dad.

Dad is the typical Italian parent – he works in the fruit game, he is loud, and loves his veggie garden. Dad was my best team mate through footy. He was goal umpire, team manager, orange peeler and my own personal coach. Footy was our thing, even though he didn't understand the game all that well in the early days but soon he became good enough to know whether I had played well or in his own words "shithouse, because you look like you can't breathe properly." For those who know Dad know that's not a dig at me or an attack of one of those abusive sporting parents. That was his way of saying "put your shoulders back, hold your head high and you won't look so shithouse." He is very big on taking pride in your personal and physical appearance.

My knee injury meant that I didn't play footy for that entire year. There was no time for Dad and me together on the weekends anymore. When I returned to play a year later I had my license and drove myself to games. Dad would then come down in his own car, watch a little bit of the game and then go back home. The change in our relationship was evident. He got on my nerves for asking the simple, petty questions. I realise now that it was his way of trying to find a way back in to reconnect with me. I was at an age when if I got injured I suppressed all feelings that weren't positive ones and hid it all under the surface. I hadn't physically lost Dad but the connection that we shared was severed and neither of us knew how to get it back, nor did we have the communication skills to speak to each other in the correct manner without it turning into a slinging match of abuse towards each other.

In the early days of my job at SEN it is fair to say my ego very quickly supersized itself to enormous proportions. There were times when I felt invincible at school, on top of the world with not a care in the world. I had a mate or knew someone at every turn of the corner and would say G'day to countless school peers throughout the entire day. When you're naturally enthusiastic and make the most of every situation I guess that tends to shine through and people want to feel that, so they will come over and say hi to chat for a few minutes. Without trying to sound arrogant I would like to add that I was known at school, I had a reputation and it felt good. It felt safe! I never set out to have an infectious personality. I find myself very fortunate that I didn't take myself or school too seriously and just enjoyed being in the surroundings of other like minded people.

Everyone I would speak to after school days would ask "how's it all going at SEN?" or remark "We always knew you'd make it with your loud voice and passion." While it was amazing to hear those things from people I grew up with, I had a brash arrogance that responded with "yeah, I knew I'd make it as well." I still hear and get these words most days of the week and I thoroughly enjoy talking to people about SEN, but I feel a sense of pride that people take interest in my life and what I'm doing, I find myself to be a bit more humble when responding to the kind things people say rather than just adding it to the ego bank and watching the ego grow.

Through my job I've met people I grew up aspiring to be and have mentors in my life that will be there forever more to push me to get the best out of myself every single day. Not a day goes by when I don't walk into work with a smile because I really do love my job. "Do what you love and you'll never work a day in your life." Every time I go into SEN I feel like that; I leave inspired to come back the next day and be better than the previous day. Little did I know at that stage that my perspective on work and life would change in the not-too-distant future!

CHAPTER 3

That nagging feeling got so strong in the days after I declined a trip to America that I was forced to sit in silence one afternoon in my bedroom. I genuinely wanted a holiday. As a 14 year old I'd travelled to parts of Europe with my family for 6 weeks and didn't have a great desire to get back there in a hurry. Through playing football for St Bernard's I was honoured to be given the chance to play for Victoria in representative footy over in New Zealand against their national side, an all expenses paid trip to Christchurch. When I got back from that trip with a bunch of new mates, I didn't think I could get a better holiday or meet a better bunch of guys. It was "the most amazing thing I've ever done" and I felt so honoured to just be nominated and then selected to play.

The other option I had was a relaxing time on a beach somewhere but again I don't have an amazing body and have no real interest in swimming in the water sipping pina coladas or anything like that. In that quiet moment of sitting there, it all came flooding back to me – trek Kokoda. Work was a challenge in itself but I felt like I'd fallen into the comfort zone; I loved every minute of it and it felt comfortable. I needed a challenge and walking Kokoda was my answer; it felt right. I'm not much of a camper. I've done it once for 3 days in 2005 and hated every single second of it at the time, yet here I was, committing to 10 days in a foreign place, in the jungle! What was I doing?

My cousin Rob was training for a 100km Oxfam walk during 2012; he'd also done a watered down version of a triathlon and had become an endurance king. I asked him whether Kokoda was something he'd done. He hadn't done it, but was very interested in the challenge for himself, so together, we signed up.

My dad always tells me that the first option is generally the best option. So when I googled up Kokoda treks, Back Track Adventures was the first link that came up, it was the first link I clicked and it was the only one I bothered with. The brochure they sent had everything I was after. I saw it was an affordable price and again, everything just fell into place. One thing I was keen on was getting myself into the best shape physically to complete this to the maximum potential that I could. I also decided that I'd like to do this without having to trudge in pouring rain all day every day, so after reading all the information, I booked for October 19, 2013, with Back Track Adventures, Team 20. That gave me 12 months to prepare myself for what I knew would be one of the biggest challenges of my life.

In my typical ways I threw everything into the

first week after booking. I was running on adrenalin and the excitement. I wanted to get to October 19 quickly. It was still 12 months ahead, so I'd quickly plateau and wasn't interested in doing the 12 months lead up work. It has become one of my usual traits to rush into something. I see the end goal, but I'm not prepared to put in the hard yards and constructive steps required before reaching the 'pinnacle'. I've worked on a couple of projects that are half finished and may never be finished because of my inability to fully complete a task. Since finishing Kokoda I have learnt more about slowing down and embracing each moment. Each task will be a successful one if you put your mind to it, be patient, and prepared to work at it, one step at a time.

In April of 2013, Rob had to pull out. He was granted an opportunity to work in Canada. When he conveyed it to me, I thought for all of half a second whether I should cancel as well but by then I realized I was hell bent on going. At that time NOTHING was going to stop me. I decided to get a copy of the movie Kokoda and I read a couple of books. I did as much as I could to get some sort of understanding of what I would experience while I was over there, which, by the way, is near on impossible! Little did I know at that stage that doing the trek on my own was the least of my worries.

CHAPTER 4

I decided that if I kept going down this track of minimal training for maximum benefits I wasn't going to get through Kokoda overly well, so I went back down to the footy club and just jumped into training a couple of nights a week to get the body moving, and to get back that social aspect I had lost through work.

In April 2013 I was introduced to John Clark; he walked into SEN from Fox Sports to take over the reigns as the breakfast producer. I was all too happy to have him! Before I met Johnny I was the one-out breakfast producer. The position was thrust upon me after spending the Christmas period doing the breakfast show. I had a week's break from early mornings before being called and told I was in charge of the breakfast show until a replacement producer was found. I did enjoy the job thoroughly but never really wanted to apply for the position to make it my very own. I had feelings and thoughts that told me I wasn't ready for this step as I had seen myself fall into a laconic state when I'd done the show previously.

Each day that passed I was adding more stress to my life, pouring more agitation into my days, adding unwanted kilos to my body and turning into someone that wasn't overly pleasant to be around. I hardly saw friends at the best of times and this made it even more difficult. Along with that I was unmotivated to "move" and "train". I would come home, go to bed for a sleep and stay in my room for most of the afternoon. My energy was dull and stagnant which most likely brought the people around me down, of course, outside of mum, dad and Lisa. No one saw that side of me. I was quite good at hiding my worries and stresses by burying them. I used humour to hide everything from the outside world.

It's fair to say that "Clarky" was a blessing that I was all too happy to embrace. From the minute we met we've clicked. He took me under his wing and signed me up at his gym where we go boxing and have done so most days of most weeks since April. Not only is it great for fitness and the ultimate sweating session. Punching a bag offered me a great release of the day's stresses and there is a great discipline in boxing that you tend to miss out when watching a highlights reel or a fight on the TV. I have no interest in fighting and will never be a fighter. Johnny taught me the values of putting everything in to a training session and leaving nothing on the sidelines.

Throw all in and when you've got nothing left, you just go again in the hope that you will find something! That little rule or motto that we tell ourselves before each session has the potential to push me to break through my comfort zone and has allowed me to grow in my training.

Countless times he pulled me up when I fell behind saying, "mate, you're doing Kokoda; you're not going to finish it by sitting on your ass at home! It's not going to make any difference to me whether you finish or not." Those little barbs that he constantly threw at me only spurred me on and made me want to succeed even more! He was the last person I texted before my adventure began, thanking him for the past few months when he pushed me to get to where I was and for inspiring me when I felt down and out for the count.

My Text to Clarky

"I'm a fucking nervous wreck here Mort. Fucking shitting myself! I need to thank you though! You probably won't like it or say did not do anything for me but you took me under your wing with boxing in the last 6 months, showed me the way to train like a boss and you got me through! You're a legend and a dumb dog all at once! In 10 days time when she's all over I'll say "ohh how good is this!" and Whooshka! We are on!!"

Clarky's response to me

"You'll be right Mort. You've done the homework, now time to pass the exam. You're fit,

it'll get done. I'm the chief dumb dog! Just listen to Rexy in your head for the week and it'll be sweet as a nut. Hurry the fuck up and get back!"

I was scared to within an inch of my life, yet his calming influence had great effect on me.

CHAPTER 5

I said I was so driven and focused to get through this Kokoda trek that NOTHING was going to stop me. All of that focus, all of that drive, all that passion came to a screeching halt when my world came crashing down on August 17, 2013.

I plummeted lower than I ever have before. I've never been confronted with death or with serious tragedy. My grandfather was killed in a tragic car accident in 1989, 12 months before I was born but otherwise I'd been on a very lucky streak and never been immediately affected as I was on that Saturday afternoon.

Christopher Lane was going for a run as he did most days. Chris was a keen baseballer and was over in the USA on a sporting scholarship, Chris was at his girlfriend's house waiting for her to come home from work. He had been back over there after his Spring Break in Australia for 3 days, all set to embark on his final year of college. Chris was a Melbourne boy, born and bred. Chris was a mad West Coast Eagle fan, and a true larrikin in every sense of the word. Chris was a Bernard's boy. Chris was my best friend!

To learn Chris had been killed in a senseless, mind numbing, cold blooded murder shook me to my core and it has every day since. Three teenagers, utterly bored one afternoon, decided they wanted to kill someone, unfortunately for all of the people that knew Chris and were touched by him directly or indirectly. Those three kids chose him. At 22 years of age, going on 23 on September 2, his life was suddenly and unexpectedly over.

It broke me; it broke all of us. There was not only an outpouring of emotion that filled Melbourne and Australia's news services but worldwide exposure for the champion kid who was humble and quiet, and would've been taken aback by all the fuss. His dad put it so well the day we were forced to say goodbye to him by saying, "To try to make sense of what has happened in this senseless tragedy is the shortest way to insanity." My best mate, with the world at his feet! All of it, taken away from him in an instant!

I met Chris in 2003 when we started our high school journey together and immediately became the best of friends. Some of the greatest memories I've got are moments with him. We were 2 typical boys growing up that loved our sport and the chance to be smartasses to anyone within ear shot of us. He was the undisputed king of quick wit with an answer for everything. 27 consecutive days in the wrong uniform at school, each day with a different forged note in his diary to explain why he had the comfort of sports gear on and the rest of us had the button up shirt and tie. They were either believable notes or by then the teachers had given up trying to discipline him or punish him in any way. To me he was a genius beyond his years at school.

He was an extremely persuasive bugger, in our early days of year 7. This was highlighted during our orientation camp. Chris was the main instigator to wake us all up and get us all out of our cabins. Once he got the first boy up, the second followed, and so on and so forth. We ran amok around the campsite that night encouraged by his ability to get out of anything. Certain students got in trouble. Laney got away with it.

Now, on to my second camping experience prior to doing Kokoda. Myself and Chris were the "footballers" in our group, so we self-nominated ourselves to lead our hike without having any idea where we were going. Everything across the first two days were going along fine until our arrogance took over, our ego of being "better" than the rest of our group causing a divide amongst us all; we got lost and were forced to bush bash our way back to the campsite on our final day of our 3 day camp. When I am looking back on it now, once I am doing Kokoda, I realize how reliant you become on your team mates out in the middle of nowhere to help you through because without them you're nothing. We obviously let our egos get the better of us on this occasion and finished with a funny story to tell but nothing to be overly proud of.

Chris' mentality was typical on this 3 day event and he had always been this way. He decided who was to carry what equipment for the journey. Because I was the "wog" of the two of us, and since the supplies we were given was pasta and sauce, he decided it was my job to cook our meals. Naturally he was the stronger of us, so he called upon himself to carry the tent. Unfortunately our theories didn't work with our food tasting crap because although I have an Italian heritage I didn't know the first thing about cooking or camping. Chris' inability to not listen during our lesson of tent building meant he had no idea what went where in the construction of the tent. Only he knows whether he bullied his cousin Zac who was with us into building it or not, but in the end our tent flooded. It was ironical really that we camped on the windiest, wettest night that has probably ever hit Victoria (That's not the case but that is how it felt!) causing us to lie there laughing about how shit we were at camping and that we would've needed a chopper to airlift us out of the Otway's back to Essendon. I'll never forget hearing him say while we were there drowning in the rain, "Pigs, it's true, I am a camper at heart; I sleep under the stars. All 5 of them from the penthouse sweet." Typical Laney! Always making light of any situation!

We never took anything seriously and apart from the serious footy discussions about why he barracked for an interstate side, we never held what may be perceived as serious, in-depth, meaningful conversations. Yet to me, our conversations were everything I loved to talk about and so did he. Things got heated from time to time and I'll never forget the year Collingwood was last on the ladder and West Coast were on top, only for the Magpies to beat them. I strolled in to school on the Monday morning all set for our AFL weekend review. I had a few little humorous one liners planned to bait Laney with throughout the day. I had barely set foot in the school ground before copping a barrage of my own from him and putting me back in my place quick smart. Maybe it was in these chats that he developed his debating skills which enabled him to spin anything into his favour and the outcome always suited Chris more than anyone else. It was all part of his charm!

In year 12, with him already locked and loaded for life after school, he "bullied" us into an idea that we wouldn't do homework in the classes that we had together (I say bullied, but we were more than happy to commit to that). English, Math and Business Studies. No homework and more free time worked for me. We signed the unwritten contract with the agreement "Less is more." That worked for him, but no well for me! The deal was that if I did homework he could punch me; I wasn't allowed to punch him though. He wrote the rules to suit him. Would you expect anything different? Somehow we got through the entire year by doing no homework (Well I did; I just believed that he did as well). I beat him by 0.5 in our VCE scores. I didn't beat him at much else, so was all too happy to bask in my glory and lap up the satisfaction. That was until he put me in the Nerd category and the gloating stopped immediately.

We never told each other how we felt, since growing boys in their teens seldom say that stuff anyway! Never. If he were here today I still probably wouldn't tell him and he wouldn't tell me how he felt, but together we both knew the love and respect we had for one another. I miss Chris every day and will forever do so. I don't think he consciously understood or realised the positive impact he had on the people he met along the way; he'd say he wasn't doing anything out of the ordinary or trying to be anything but himself. I always felt I could stand up, aim for the sky, and in his presence, I'd be able to reach it. If only I can be half the person that he was in the way he interacted with people, in the way he threw everything he had into every day, and in the way he lived his short but spectacular life! Then I know I'm well on my way to a successful future and a life that I'll one day look back on and be proud of.

On August 19 the story had filtered through the media and was front page news of all Melbourne papers and the lead story on all news services. I was given the opportunity on SEN to chat about Chris and somehow, managed to put a few words together. I was very honoured to have been given that chance to speak in such high regard of Laney. But at the time it was the hardest thing I had ever done. The amount of support I received from people who heard the few minutes on SEN was phenomenal. I had an overwhelming feeling that somehow, in a helpless situation, I felt my contribution helped a little.

I collect and store all sorts of quotes in an album, from inspiration to imagination, and everything in between. One of the first ones I ever saved was "You don't know how strong you are, until being strong is the only choice you have."

When I got that call from Clarky at 6.30am on Monday, August 19, I didn't think I had any strength or could possibly get a single word out, but something in me spurred me on. I did not want to have the sense of regret that I missed out on speaking about the great man and was simply trying to put into words the type of person that was so senselessly taken from this world. It was the least I could do for the kid who did so much for me in my development.

In the few days after Chris' death, the rallying of friends and support from all angles was evident. No one wanted to leave anyone alone or feel they were going through this alone. Each year throughout high school we sat through the final year 12 assembly always hearing the school captain say the same thing over and over, "Once a

Bernards boy, always a Bernards boy." While it may be clichéd, nothing has ever rung truer than those few words. I have a great sense of pride in being one of those Bernards boys and have never taken for granted the opportunities I was given through my time at St Bernards.

Dealing with a tragedy such as this has forced me to have feelings and emotions that I've never experienced before. I've done a lot of counselling work ever since, using that as an outlet. I've worked on meditating daily and praying to the higher self more than ever. I've had insights and visions that have come to me in the form of "answers". I was shown a period of our teens, once again at our year 9 camp where we spent the afternoon surfing on the beach. I don't do the beach very well, nor do I have any interest in surfing at all. Again, it was something that was out of my comfort zone. I was hesitant to get out there and give it a go. I reluctantly did it and after 15 minutes I got hit in the head with Laney's surfboard; it was the perfect excuse to get out of the water and sit on the sand to watch the rest of my class mates surf, which I opted to do. The message that came through while I sat in my counselling session explaining this story was to "Never Give Up." Don't give up on anything or anyone, because you just never know what is around the corner; the miracle could be moments away.

Chris gave me the thrill of living; he was one of the reasons I got out of bed every morning and raced to school all set for another day of fun and frivolity. When we played footy he made me feel as if I were 6 feet tall and capable of anything. The inspiration I got just from being in his presence made me a better person. I don't know if Chris lived by a motto or a quote but "You get the best out of others when you get the best out of you" may well have been the motto for Chris Lane. He definitely got the best out of me and most likely of anyone else who walked into his path. A special kid with the biggest heart.

The last time I saw Chris was in mid-July 2012. It was an unexpected last meeting. He was in Melbourne on Spring break. Collingwood were playing Geelong that Saturday night at the MCG but instead of going to the game I chose to go out to see a friend perform in a music concert and the plan was to head out to a nightclub after that with a few other mates. It got to around 2am in the morning, so I decided it was time to pack it up, pack it in, and head home. As I stumbled out of the club and onto the street, across the road I heard "Piggggzzzzzz mate!" There he was. In the middle of the city. Laney! All the way from the USA! I can still feel my excitement levels at seeing him in the most unexpected of places. Instead of going home, his persuasive manner and the fact that I hadn't seen him in a while caused me to stay out with him. I had promised Mum I would be home by 2.30am/3am at the latest, my phone battery did not have enough charge lest to telephone her. We decided that from where we were we would go to the Casino and try to win some money.

We were literally a 3 minute walk away from Crown in a sober state. Since we were drunk, we lost all sense of direction and no cab would pick us up because we were far too close to the casino and it wouldn't be worth their while. We took left turns and right turns, and went up and down the wrong streets, all the while not really caring where we were going; just enjoying each other's company more than anything. Chris found a cab parked on the side of the road with its hazard lights on. We stopped him to ask him for a ride home, but he refused to take us anywhere because the car was broken down. Laney went around the front of the cab, took a photo of the number plate and berated the cabbie saying, "I'm reporting you in the morning! You're not allowed to refuse entry, but you're refusing entry. I'm reporting this." Eventually a cab stopped for us after 45 minutes of whistling at them. The taxi dropped me off first; Laney "shouted" me for it. It was about 5am when I finally walked in the door. As quietly as I could I went straight to bed praying Mum wasn't up to kill me for being so late. Thankfully she wasn't, but when I woke up a couple of hours later she was. I decided to just tell her the truth and let whatever happen, happen. As soon as I mentioned I was out with Chris I noticed her mood change; she asked how he was and we ended up chatting for a while about the great man.

At the time I took that moment for granted, as I'm sure most other people would as well. Throughout the last few months it has been one of the most cherishable moments I have with Chris and one that I definitely will never forget. I've had the feeling of heaviness and being sick in the pit of my stomach with that being the last time I saw him and as I mentioned before' I never got that chance to tell him how I really feel, but we never did. It is a regret that I now have but I think about that night now with the greatest smile and the happiest of thoughts. Chris and I, doing what we loved best—being boys!

A fund was set up online for people to donate money towards to help; the hope was to raise $15,000. That amount was reached within the first hour of being set up. It literally skyrocketed and went far beyond expectations. Through SEN we managed to get it up on the big screen of the MCG during Friday night footy, ironically—the game being played was between Collingwood and West Coast (our teams). The ripple effect of his passing was felt around the entire country and around the world, amidst all of this tragedy and pain. My mate, Chris Lane, had gone global!

A few days after Chris' death my final payment to my Kokoda experience was due. I vividly remember having made the decision that I couldn't go through with this trek and I was all set to pull out. After all, I seemed to be coping well with this tragedy compared to a few of my other mates. I wanted to be there for them through all of this, and offer them the support I thought they needed. Little did I know at the time that it was I who was crying out for support and help to get through the struggles of that loss.

Nothing was going to stop me from doing this, except for the one thing that no one could've ever anticipated happening. I was all set to cancel; it was August 21 at 1.30pm. The phone was ringing and I knew what I was going to say. I was all set to explain the situation that I found myself in. Not that it was about money at all but I was hopeful I could get the money I had already outlaid back and put my trip on hold for another time.

In the few seconds after the lady from Back Track had answered my mood changed. I started out explaining that I was dealing with a tragedy and personal issues, but instead of cancelling and pulling out, I stumbled over asking if I could postpone my payments, and passed into whipping out my MasterCard and paying for the remainder of the trip. I still don't know what persuaded me to pay instead of cancelling. I've often thought that Laney was in the room with me and gave me the little nudge that I needed to break through my comfort zone to achieve the goal I'd set for myself.

If he was, I believe he knew in himself that I could accomplish this, or from above he wanted to watch me stumble, bumble and struggle through 10 days in the jungle for his own entertainment! I think on this occasion, I'll go with the latter! Typical Laney!

All I know is, whatever be the reasons for choosing to pay, I've not regretted it for an instant, from the minute I hung up the phone until the second my feet hit the ground at Melbourne. airport upon completion my Kokoda trip which was dedicated to Christopher Lane xxox.

CHAPTER 6

October 18, 2013. The day my Kokoda adventure began. We didn't officially start the trek until October 20 but I had connecting flights from Melbourne to Sydney to PNG. I was in such a state of disillusion and excitement that I completely disregarded everything and all I wanted to do was start walking to soak up the experience of everything that Kokoda had to offer.

When people go on holidays they generally need to get "last minute" items; they are common in every holiday kit taken away, aren't they? Unless it means me! All my "last minute" items included packing my bag to trek with, cleaning my boots, trying to find my torch, unpack my bag because there were irrelevant items in there and re-pack the bag. Oh, and go to the doctors for one final check-up.

As if my nerves hadn't already kicked in by then! I so desperately wanted to get on the plane to Sydney so that I could be alone with my thoughts and take in the gravity of what was about to unfold. However, doctors, bloody hell! I genuinely appreciate everything the Docs do for people; they're brilliant and their job is relentless. But are you guys in any danger, any bloody danger of a little bit of positivity in your position?

I should explain something my T20 team mates and parents know. That is, I don't like needles at all! I inquired about needles in September for walking the Kokoda track. I was told, with the climate being the way it is during the time I was there, they weren't necessary. That was music to my ears, so I didn't bother following up that for more information. I took that as a chance to escape that step in the process. I was a mix of excited emotions and panic type nerves right up until the day I was leaving when the Doctor rattled off the 4 or 5 needles required prior to going to PNG, as well as malaria tablets. Are you mocking me Doc? Way to add even more nerves and fear?

I left the doctors with a packet of tablets with little yellow beads in there, looking disgraceful. I was to take one a day until the bottle was finished; that was to be until around the middle of November. In short, on the 10 days I was trekking. 6 tablets were consumed and then, in typical fashion that wouldn't surprise anyone who knows me, I left the bottle of tablets in my hotel room and they never made it back to Australia.

I still like to think I'm the winner out of that little "battle" with the docs; I got through unscathed with no malaria or any issues that the needles would've fought off! Mind you, if I was to do this trip again or was to recommend it to anyone, it's best to go through the full process and eliminate any of the worries that I had the day I was leaving.

Once my bag was finally packed, I was ready to head to Melbourne Airport and start the adventure. Not before a few overwhelming tears. Saying goodbye to my Dad was incredibly hard; my parents had been on holidays overseas before while I stayed at home. Same as my sister (who travelled Europe earlier in 2013), yet it was never the other way around.

I always see people at the airport saying goodbye to loved ones in tears and I would think, "come on fellas, get a grip on yourself." This is the result of suppressing any feelings or emotions throughout my years of growing up. I had shut down that side of me completely and only had humour. I always thought the goodbyes at the airport were cute and nice but I never considered for a second to express those thoughts verbally as I did not consider that as a very manly thing to do. Now it was my turn; the tears came and flowed freely. As if the doctors weren't already overwhelming enough, there were thoughts that this could be my final goodbye from everything I had ever known. Turns out it was. In a physical sense I came back a few kilograms lighter but the impact on me was very strong emotionally and mentally; yes I definitely did come back with a completely different mindset.

As I got into the car with Mum who was to drop

me off at the airport, there was a note on the seat from my sister Lisa. We have never been all that close, usually at each other's throats and not getting along all that often. We usually come together at dinner time to take the piss out of Mum and Dad to give ourselves a laugh but otherwise it's usually a battle for who gets to spend more time in the bathroom and which bedroom is the cleaner of the 2.

I hadn't been able to finish reading the note she wrote me, not because I didn't want to but at the time, I just couldn't finish it without breaking down. I carried the note in my pocket my entire trip and it now sits safely in my Go Pro case.

Hello fat boy slim
I couldn't get you anything to take (You ate it already) and mum said you don't have room. So I'm sending you off with a nice little poem

You were once all alone
Until came Lisa trying to be your clone
And it was the best present ever
To have a little sister who's actually quite clever
I know you love me more, every single day
But you think you're cooler and I'm gay
That's not true, I'm the baby girl
And one day you'll buy me a twirly whirl
I'm always fat and food comes first
Even though I'm dying of thirst
For some coca cola in a pepsi glass

We both know it won't help my ass
Thanks for reading my attempt at a poem, for you Mr Pig. Also known as ham
A quote from you now
"I don't give a damn"

I hope you have the absolute time of your life on this trip, I have no doubt it'll be one of the hardest things you do, but we all know you'll smash through any challenge like a boss! If you ever start feeling shit or anxious (I'm the queen of that shit) just remember your baby sister almost beat Europe's ass all alone!
Don't eat too much plane food, they feed you non-stop and you'll break their toilet!
Love you always and always and always, I'll be bored shitless without you for 12 days, not 2 weeks!!! xoxoxox

When I landed in Sydney, I turned on my phone to countless messages from Mum, Dad, Lisa and friends saying "good luck", plenty of well wishes and a couple that simply said go get em'; it all gave me a great sense of satisfaction and gratitude. I felt honoured to be representing so many people and having all that support behind me only spurred me on further.

I went to sleep that night in Sydney without the knowledge that the next day could well be one of the greatest days of my life.

CHAPTER 7

October 19, 2013. My flight from Sydney airport to PNG according to my itinerary was to be at 9.45am. I set my alarm for 6.45am but woke up well before that time. I went downstairs to the breakfast buffet thinking about stocking up on one last meal before I headed off. I managed to stomach a piece of toast and a sip of tea; nothing was going down that could settle the nerves.

When I walked into Sydney airport, I noticed I had stuffed up my flight times (naturally, that was bound to happen). So I was there an hour early because the itinerary was working on Brisbane time which was an hour behind Melbourne and Sydney. I eventually checked in and headed straight down to the gate that I was set to board from, a million questions running through my head. All fairly negative and worrying ones; the main one was if I was ever going to make it back home to Melbourne and see my family again.

Each time I thought about my family while sitting there I would start to well up and cry. I still hadn't met any of the people on my team. I was sitting at the ass end of Sydney airport, vulnerable, lonely and all alone.

I was absolutely terrified and tried to think of any

excuse to get through the next 10 days as fast as possible to get back home. I thought about the last group of Bernards boys that did the trek a couple of months earlier, convincing myself that 10 days is a short space of time. I would be home before I knew it and back into life at SEN. Though I said all that in the negative space, the flip side was I was still moving forward. I had all the support in the world, I was smashing through my comfort zone beyond belief, and I was developing from a boy to a man before my own eyes. This was my right of passage. It was not as though this moment had crept up on me; I had 12 months to prepare for it. Yet here I was overwhelmed and excited all at once.

I had bought a book at Melbourne Airport, Leigh Matthews' (The greatest player in AFL / VFL history) *Accept the Challenge*. I put on Facebook in a status moments before I left that it was in fact "Challenge Accepted", come hell or high water; I was going to take on Kokoda and I was going to win.

That wave of excited emotion had disappeared as I sat there with my book and my glasses on hiding the tears of fear that I had. And then out of nowhere, a voice came. I was greeted by a voice. Someone was talking to me. With the same kind of t-shirt . She was a total stranger to me. She is now one of the most amazing and special individuals that I have the privilege of calling my dear friends.

Renea Clements was the first of my T20 team mates that I met and have enjoyed her company ever since. She had a calming influence on me amidst all of my pent up emotion and that was extremely helpful. There were 8 amazing people from Newcastle all on the journey for the Westpac Helicopter Rescue Service and I was introduced to them all instantly after saying hello to Renea.

My fears and worries disappeared as soon as I got chatting to a few of them. Without realising I had my Collingwood shorts on, I spent the next 10-15 minutes waiting for the plane in a bit of light hearted banter about Australian football, how good AFL (Australian Football League) is compared to the NRL (National Rugby League). The usual banter followed, "Sydneysiders and their one-eyed rubbish sport, there's only one good NRL team and that's the Melbourne Storm!"

CHAPTER 8

Without a doubt Renea Clements has been one of the most influential females that have come into my life, right behind my very own mother who has guided me through everything.

In the similar mould to Mum, Renea voluntarily took on that "motherly" role to me while out in the jungle and continues to do so. How fortunate and grateful I am to have a mate like Chris, a loving and caring mother like mine with lots of support and now a new bond with someone just as incredible, displaying all the qualities that all of us aspire to have.

I thought I had the inspiration and drive to complete this trek, but here was a single mother of 3 amazing young boys. It was a treat to look into her eyes and hear her voice when she talked with such passion about Mason, Rhys and Cooper; I hear the same from my own mother. There seems to be a great sense of pride that comes with being a parent and achieving the ultimate in proving to your own children that anything really is possible. Renea carried hopes and dreams as big as the world itself. To hear her talk about her dreams, wants and needs was phenomenal; here I was listening to a like-minded person who would stop at nothing until she reached her innermost happiness. Just like Chris she spurred on those feelings and emotions I got from spending time with Laney, waking up each morning with a smile feeling a sense of greatness and importance, and throwing everything possible into the coming day.

Throughout the 10 days out on the track she would constantly check up on me to make sure I was coping okay. I was a disorganised nightmare some days with items from my bag lying all over the campsite we would stay in for the night. I've never enjoyed playing UNO with someone as I did with Renea, being able to beat her and watch her trying to cheat to get an advantage; but it's impossible to beat a cheater at his own game.

There is one very humorous memory from the track with Renea that stands out, on the final morning of our trek, as if I hadn't done enough memorable, silly, stupid things already. I decided it would be hilarious to unpin her tent while she was in it. I didn't realise she was in the middle of getting changed. Luckily for her, I didn't have my eye contacts in, which meant things were blurry already and I stuffed up the unpinning of the tent so that it was an average practical joke at best. As I scampered back into my tent, some goodie-goodie wanna-be teacher's pet dobbed me in to Renea and while I was in mine sorting out my life in a bag and putting my contacts in, my tent collapsed around me, not just the roof or the front door but the whole thing – unpinned, unchained, flattened! The ultimate payback. A taste of my own medicine. If only I let her win one game of UNO!

I guess it can be hard to get a gauge and really get to know a person within 10 days, especially when for a few hours in the day you're walking in a straight line, head down, trying to keep your footing on the most difficult terrain on the planet so that there isn't much chatter. Yet I got the privilege of getting to know Renea during our down time and I couldn't be more grateful that most days since the completion of our adventure we've got to know each other even more and the connection we have has become even stronger. There are only ever 3 certainties in life – that you're born, that you die and that you pay taxes – but I'm in an extremely breathtaking position to add a fourth certainty to my list – Renea Clements, a friend for life.

The friendship that we have is more than just that of a "How are you going mate" kind of association. It's pretty much open, no topic is off limits and complete honesty is the only rule. I've opened up about things I never would've imagined I'd talk to anyone about. On the surface I'm a smartass, carefree, easy going kid. Renea pushed me to show so much more, to go underneath the outside personality, and allowed me to be the deep thinker that I sometimes am.

I've fallen on hard times since returning from Kokoda, but apart from the hours of support my parents put in for me, Renea has been there for me throughout every minute of every day. No problem is too big or too small to talk about, no time of the day or night is an inconvenience and it is a true testament to the type of person that she is. I'm continually inspired throughout our conversations. I have a great deal of admiration for the person that she is and she's unknowingly a mentor of mine for the rest of my life. (Once she reads this, she'll know though!)

Likewise with other members of T20, there are memories and moments I've had with Renea that I will cherish forever and will never get tired of reliving them with her and talking about our amazing experiences that occurred in what really is one of the most magical places on earth.

CHAPTER 9

After flying to PNG with the T20 members from Newcastle, there were only two members of our team I have left to meet. I was told they were two men from Queensland and I left it at that. When we got to the Holiday Inn I raced straight up to my room to get hold of the wifi, to send a message to my parents to let them know I was there safely. I sat there in my room all alone cried my heart out again. The fear I had was so overwhelming for me; there was real concern about what the bloody hell I was doing! Nothing I said, did or thought seemed to overcome the fear, so I stayed in my room for as long as possible.

We were due to have an "induction meeting" at 4pm down at the bar; I stayed up in my room and was the last one down there, telling my group that I was upstairs sleeping when really I was so scared to move. Down at the bar I was introduced to Mark Wharton and Dave "Trace" Austin.

There were 2 guys who had been at the bar for a couple of hours already enjoying PNG's finest brew. At first glance they were your stereotypical mates whom you'd see at any pub around Australia, enjoying the company of each other. Little did I realise at that time that those guys would take me under their wing and were literally in my shadow every step of the way on the track. That overwhelming fear I had disappeared when I got chatting to them both across our final dinner before the trek started.

I saw everything that I had with Chris in Mark and Trace, including the constant banter, and the ability to take the piss out of you and each other was great fun. "If you can't have a laugh at yourself then you're probably in the wrong group." I'd established a relationship with two guys I'd met only a couple of hours earlier yet it was as if we knew each other our whole life. We hadn't even started walking and they had passed advice on to me about taking some gear out of my bag and leaving it at the hotel to make my gear a little lighter. It was full of unnecessary items and clothing that was not required to trek the jungle. That night I hung on to every word knowing these guys had the experience on their side and any advice was good advice that was worth listening too.

Renea took the role of mother to me, while Mark and Trace combined had the position of father, and didn't they succeed! Every morning I woke up to hear Mark tell me the clothing number he'd be trekking in for the day – "blue t-shirt, with the black shorts, the gators because he was feeling sexy and the brown walking boots" only to cross over to Trace to get one of life's greatest theories and to realize why things are the way they are.

Our conversations during the trekking was stuff you'd hear over the drip tray at a BBQ and they ramped up even more when we were sitting around the table for what had become the most cherishable conversations I've ever been a part of.

I mentioned they were in my shadow for much of the trip. It was established on Day one that because I was the only person in my group to not have a porter and was carrying my own pack, I'd lead from the front. The rest of the group settled in behind me. I was conscious of being the leader; I wanted to be at the front because I knew if I was near the back I'd probably fall behind and still be walking. As early as on Day two, I was feeling a little light-headed and decided I'd hold off from being at the front for a half hour or so and walk in the middle. It was the one and only time I wasn't at the front. While you are at the front, everything is in front of you and you pretty much control the pace of the group. The middle got a bit stagnant at times with people in front trying to work out where to step or stopping for a Kodak photo moment.

I was still in a moment of impatience because I just wanted to hurry up and get to the next rest stop for a break. Michelle stopped in front of me for a quick snap. Here was my chance to pass and get into the group of front-runners. I stood on a rock and was quickly tumbling, flipped off the side of a cliff and down the embankment. My bag pulled me a fair way down and I felt as though I just kept rolling and rolling. The story quickly ended up going something like this: "I fell off a cliff, went 450m down, dislocated a shoulder, snapped my achilles, saw God at the bottom, climbed back to the top and then powered on through." Unfortunately the glamorous story never really got any traction and the truth is that my bag probably saved my life. I got just a scratch under my left shoulder while the biggest thing to bruise was my ego.

From that moment, no one would trust me to walk anywhere else in the line except up the front. Mark and Trace decided they were most suitable to follow in second position and came up with "Joe Duty". They were within arm's length the entire time to grab hold of my straps for the eventuality when I went sliding again and keep me basically from killing myself. Each day I grew a little bit more confident in my hiking ability. I began to embrace the challenges, log hopping became enjoyable and being able to pirouette in the mud and slush was great fun.

Apart from all the amazing scenery and the precious moments that we experienced, Mark, Trace and I quickly embraced every bit of food that was on offer to us. We crowned T20 a champion team and set about doing everything that a champion team should do. So porridge, cornflakes and damper in the morning became the

"Breakfast of Champions". 2 minute noodles, tuna and crackers became the "Lunch of Champions" and the amazing spread at the end of a long day walking became the "Dinner of Champions". As if that wasn't special enough, mid-way through our trek, sliced cheese turned up on the lunch menu and through inquisitive minds we developed our own signature dish – "Biscuit, cheese, spam, biscuit." In the early phase, while we were concocting our meal plan for the day, I really struggled to put it together and would go "Biscuit, spam, cheese, biscuit" that was unacceptable in Mark's eyes and I was relegated from head chef back to a standard kitchen hand until I was capable of performing under the stresses of providing for T20.

For us, there was another thing that became a staple in our diet – breakfast, lunch, afternoon tea, dinner. If you're going to eat in luxury like we were, then you're going to need something to wash all that down with. That was "Number 1 Tea" – not number 1 in a ranking; it was called "Number 1 tea", and let me tell you, that is definitely not false advertising! PNG's finest tea leaves for us, liquid gold, and it was like kids at Christmas when the pot of scalding, hot water came over with the most recognisable little box that contained the number 1. I don't think boredom had set in; I was just naturally excited to promote a cup of number 1 and pushed all of T20 to have a cup of it in their hand throughout our breaks in walking. Here was

my chance to use my "commercial radio" skills to promote a pointless brand that quickly became the greatest thing on earth.

It's literally impossible not to have fun and a good time when you're surrounded with people who display such a positive nature. You're literally forced into enjoying yourself because it is one of the only ways to combat the heaviness and gravity of what you hear and go through as you're walking along the track. You make your own fun and that is the true beauty of it, especially when everyone in the group is on the same page and willing to get involved.

One afternoon I decided that when we got to camp I'd open up "Happy Hour at the Bar." The Porters arranged a couple of pots (of water) and I was offering free number 1 tea for the afternoon over a game of UNO and some table almonds on the side. While the few of us rested up "in the bar" the others were out on the grass playing soccer with the local kids and having the time of their lives. In that moment I felt as if I'd found myself; I knew why I was there and had a quiet moment of gratitude for being put in that position. We were still a few days away from finishing our trek but I thought back to a week earlier when I had been so overwhelmed and shattered. I couldn't believe the stark contrast within myself and I've got Mark, Trace, Renea and the rest of T20 to thank for that.

But they also added the world's greatest stress by all becoming a part of the greatest prank I've ever been involved in; this time however, the joke was on me.

Renea wasn't the only one to pick up my items at camp each morning; everyone did. I had stuff everywhere. There are towels, Gatorade powder, socks and a 5L can of Bushman's lying dormant on the track still, and if anyone found them I'd collect them all back with thanks. Naturally, my disorganised nature meant that it didn't come as any surprise to my team when I told them I hadn't had any needles prior to leaving for PNG.

Mark and Trace hatched a brilliant plan. They told me that without those needles I wasn't getting back into Australia and would be stuck in customs with some serious explaining to do. All that freaked me out but I initially thought surely they were pulling my leg. However, when Frank and Pete, the oldest 2 guys on the trip, agreed with them I thought I was in real trouble there and spent every night for the rest of the trip trying to think of a brilliant excuse to get back into Australia with the greatest ease. They had me believe that everyone got a yellow card before departing PNG that the Doctor ticked off and then when you got back home you would hand the card in and then you go onward to home. Obviously, no needles for me meant no card. For everyone reading this, there's no card at all. Ever!

They maintained this along the entire trip and I was getting a ribbing the whole time. While I still laughed about all of it and enjoyed the banter, there was a part of me every night that thought I was stuffed there, for good! When we finished the trek and sat back at the bar, Trace told me that through his connections he had spoken to the embassy, and all I had to do was tell the truth and then I would be fine (all of this a total load of shit!).

My flight home from PNG was very early on Tuesday, October 29. Mark and Trace weren't on our flight, but they've heard about my reaction later. While in the line they handed out a YELLOW CARD that we were required to fill in and give to customs. Things were starting to tick over in my mind, so I asked again if this was the yellow card they were talking about the whole time. It wasn't; it just coincidentally happened to be yellow. Finally, Renea pulled out her passport to show me the YELLOW CARD was the Visa everyone needed! I had one of those! When I finally realised I'd been strung along the whole time, I actually swore quite so much, yet I was very impressed with the ability of a practical joke to go for as long as it did. Only Mark and Trace were able to concoct, maintain and pull off something like this.

There were so many more moments with these 2

guys that I could go on and elaborate with, and people who have had the Kokoda experience will understand that there are just so many that there's no possible way to put them into context that would allow me to do the moment justice.

To Mark and Trace, thank you. "My ass was grass and the rest of T20 were lawnmowers" was Mark's favourite comment to me, and Trace had a theory on why that was the case.

CHAPTER 10

I've spoken about the build up to Kokoda and I've spoken about the few people that had the biggest influence on my time while I was there. Now it's time to talk about the track itself.

It is gruelling, it is intense, it has been known to break people in the past and from the first step right through until the last you can certainly see why. Our journey was from Kokoda through to Owers Corner. The first day trekking was pretty much all flat level walking and you will get to camp on the first night confident in your mind that you'll be able to get through this. The first day is supposedly a little "teaser" of what to expect, if that's the case, but then they need to re-assess the brochure. The flat spots are few and far between. They're a bit like emotions and feelings, and the ups and downs of each climb exemplify in a physical sense the battle you face sometimes in your mind.

We seemed to start each day with a "hill climb." The term 'hill' here is a complete understatement, because when you're standing at the bottom looking up it is basically a cliff face that just goes and goes and goes ever up.

It is a great way to physically see what can happen

in one's mind if they're dealing with issues. The hills are the blocks, negative debris, that are in the way. The only way to get past is to walk through and confront the negativity head on. Surely you will slip on a tree root or slide backwards momentarily, but the relentless support of others (team mates) will pick you back up and put you on the path again. There are little openings during hill climbs, maybe 15-20m of flat ground that give you enough chance to have a sip of water and then it's back to it. In fact that is the little moment you get that spurs you on to keep going because you know you're on the right track (pardon the pun). When you reach the top of the hills, throw your bag down and look at the most breathtaking views and clearings. That's the sense of relief that you've made it!

All that gruelling strain to get every little bit out of you while climbing, and constantly looking up and seeing more tree roots and steps you need, can certainly stuff you around mentally, but when you get to the top, all that pain immediately washes away and you look back down to where you started with a great sense of pride and satisfaction. I took great pleasure in reaching the top of each climb at the front, not because I had the chance to say that I was first, but because I was able to put my bag down, celebrate a little win with the team mates that were up the front with me, and then get back down the hill to support the rest of my group through.

Kokoda is something that each person has their own personal reasons for conquering. If you're selfish and self-centred out there, I don't think you'll be able to finish the journey; if you do finish in that mindset you may not get that same satisfaction out of it as you would if you were selfless and giving. I was conscious of this the whole time, Mark, Trace, Ian and Renea all behind me pushing me to the top. It was only fair that we went back down to clap and cheer the rest of our group through to finish as one. After all, that is what a champion team does!

There were times on the "hills" where there was complete silence from the group and everyone had the train out, the engine blowing, battling with the difficulty of just putting one foot in front of the other. However, at other times, we were charging up to the top with seamless ease, playing trivia games, telling jokes, laughing along the way.

Remember that what comes up must come down. So while it was gruelling to get up, coming down was far from a synch. I had Mark or Trace's hand on my bag the whole time. If I didn't know any better I'd say they were trying to push me down hill just to see me fall so that they could have a laugh, but they assure me that they were complying with the rules of "Joe Duty" and holding on for dear life so that I didn't fall!

I've had the pleasure of winning Grand Finals in a team sport and I've been a leader while playing footy, but in this team, we were all leaders and at the same time we were all invaluable team mates to each other. It is truly magical to see 12 people who don't know a great deal about each other before starting becoming the best of friends 10 days later and getting compelled to say some hard goodbyes.

CHAPTER 11

Now on to my cliff fall! Everyone got a great deal of joy out of it once we all knew that I was okay and my ego had borne the major brunt of the damage. It was in that moment that everyone realised the importance of safety and decided to support one another out on the track.

Everyone but me had a porter who was there the whole way with them. But my fall had all of them stop what they were doing and jump down the side of the cliff to my aid. They were extremely valuable and their help was priceless. Not only was there admirable selflessness, but those young men seemed so happy too. They literally had nothing but they made the most out of everything and every day.

They helped us along the way, opened up to us and had fun with us. T20 was an all inclusive group and no one was left out on their own. They even sang for us in the most harmonious melody I have ever heard. Just the pure magic in their voices was enough to move me and make me feel incredible warmth that I guess everyone gets when they hear a beautiful piece of music.

During the journey each one of us went through our own "down" moments, going back into our shells to get a grasp of the gravity of the particular situation we were faced with. However, no one seemed to be down for very long. I found myself very fortunate that I was put with people who knew how to knock the negativity out of you and make you focus on the positive, no matter how hard the challenge seemed.

I've been asked since returning whether it was physically taxing; I didn't feel so personally. I can't speak for a few of the group who were a little bit older than me, but I found it mentally taxing. Here we are walking; all of a sudden we come to a stop and are shown a rock or a tree that's just staying there. Then we were told that up in a certain tree nearby was a Japanese sniper, or on that very rock a brother stayed with his younger sibling, with gunfire going on all around them, in the final moments of his life before he died reminiscing about their childhood. I just couldn't imagine that in this magical, tranquil jungle such horror and tragedy went on some years before.

Each night was another opportunity to sit around the campfire and debrief about our interpretations of the day we'd just had. Although the serious conversation never extended into too much depth or for very long it definitely helped unwinding with people who had just experienced it rather than trying to explain the feelings and emotions that each situation brought up, because sometimes there are no words.

I spent my teenage years growing up with phones, iPads, computers, social media and the internet. There is none of that on Kokoda. No radio, no newspapers, and no contact with the outside world except for the people that you're trekking with. I learnt to value once again the importance of communication. Not texting or emailing, but sitting down with someone and getting to know them face to face. You're forced into a situation where unless you're a monk and comfortable with complete silence, you need to get through 10 days with "strangers", but you quickly realise that they're in fact not strangers at all but the best people you need to get through that situation with (well, mine were anyway). I noticed how much happier and content you can be with yourself by simply extending a hand and having a conversation by getting to know someone else.

I loved talking to them all about what drives them to get up each morning, what their personal reasons were for being here, what was on their bucket list going forward, and what steps they put in place to change their world for the better. Having worked in radio, talking is obviously a hobby of mine, so I had no problem chatting about my own trials and tribulations but I genuinely took interest in as many angles of other people as I could. I took every chance to chat and ask questions of others because I was so desperate to make the most of every minute I had out there.

Finding Myself

Remember the kid who was scared and crying in his room at the Holiday Inn on Day 1? I don't.

You can't go through a place like this and not experience and feel the magic of the place. I was pushed every minute of every day to go beyond my comfort zone and smash through every single pain barrier that I'd put up. I felt an obvious growth within myself every day and it was all unfolding in front of my very eyes. There are moments that will leave you in awe. You will be left breathless at some of the views that you see along with some of the greatest feelings and emotions that you will ever experience.

I don't know if there'll ever be another thing in this world that will replicate the thrill you get from doing Kokoda. You're not walking on a tightrope over the Grand Canyon, staring death in the face or anything like that but what you are doing is living! And there's no greater thrill in life than living and living consciously.

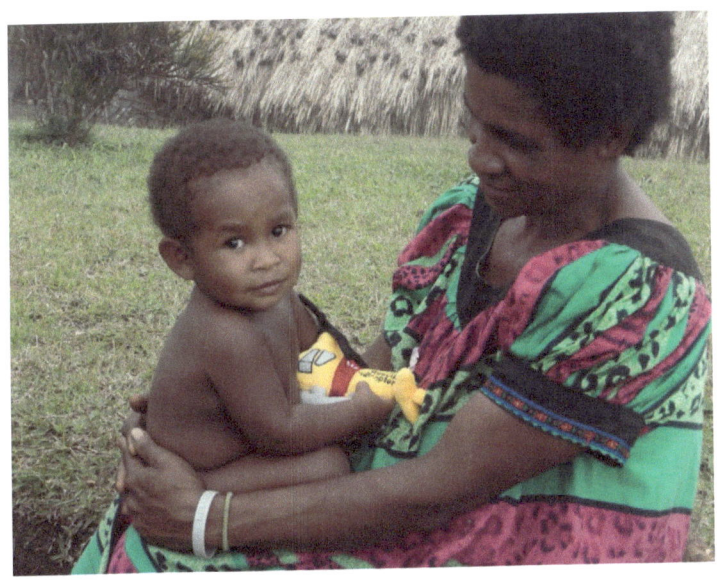

CHAPTER 12

I was completely dedicated to my job at SEN prior to the day of Chris' death, August 17, 2013 and then to doing Kokoda. I made whatever sacrifice I had to because I wanted to get ahead. I've given up playing footy and nights out with friends to chase my dream of making it to the top in my chosen field.

Yet I've come back and from those values I learnt over in PNG, I know that work is not the be all and end all in this life. It is a means to an end and always helps financially.

You yourself are the most important thing in your life. That's not to sound selfish, if you are unable to help yourself then how can you truly help someone else. The support of other people is immense, amazing and extraordinary, especially if you're open to letting people in and being strong enough to ask for help. There is no shame in asking because there are people out there who want to help you to reach your full potential. Sometimes they're able to see it a lot more clearly than you are.

Nowadays work is exactly that, work. Me succeeding in life is my dream and goal. I want that for myself and I want to express that to others.

My fellow trekkers, they were inspiring, every single one of them—Renea, Mark, Trace, Michelle, Ian, Mark, Frank, Chad, Pete, Zach, James and John. Each had their own reasons and stories for taking this journey on. I have a level of satisfaction and great pride in calling these 12 people my dear friends and I know I can call on them whenever things get rough for me and they wouldn't hesitate in extending their hand to help.

That's the sort of thing Kokoda will do for people; it epitomises everything that happened there years earlier, the coming together of Australians from all parts of the country, sticking together to fight against the Japanese to give us the special freedoms and luxuries we enjoy together. 12 of us came together between October 19 and October 29, 2013 and we will have a bond that ties us together forever.

CHAPTER 13

Our final day on the track was a day of mixed emotions for me. I was only a few hours away from completing the biggest challenge I had ever set myself, yet in the same breath I was down because it was all about to be over and back home to Melbourne was where I was headed. I wasn't sure how I'd react when it was all over; I honestly hadn't given it much thought. I wanted to enjoy each moment that came along and not think too far ahead or look too far back. We got down to our final river crossing which was significant in itself, because once through it then it was perceived we were on the "home straight" – home straight at Kokoda means another bloody hill by the way!

Down at the river I took the opportunity to have one final moment of madness, do a couple of flips off some rocks into the most beautiful running water stream, without much care for my safety. The porters were doing it and no one else wanted to jump at the chance, so I did! Why not, if it was going to end soon, it might as well end in style.

I can still put myself in those last moments of our final stretch on the track. I've never chatted as much, just saying "nearly there, not far away now", and then we got to the top. I'm not sure if it was "heaven on earth" and the landmark there was the "pearly white gates," but it felt bloody good to finish! I'd done it! Hugs, high fives and a million photos went around. Such was the high we were all on that it wouldn't have surprised anyone that we could've turned around and gone back the other way quite easily. Clearly I wasn't the only one that didn't want this journey to finish just yet.

There was still one moment to go that I had no idea about; in all of my research prior to leaving I'd forgotten or overlooked maybe the most significant piece of Kokoda – the cemetery of our fallen soldiers.

Every step I had taken on the track which in total was over 400,000 and maybe even more, I had stepped with the thought of Chris in my mind and heart. I was filled with pride and love for my best mate when I crossed that finish line, blowing a kiss up to the sky and pointing towards the heavens for my mate. On night 8 we were asked to go around and give our reasons for doing Kokoda, it's not my place to divulge what any of my team mates reasons were, but I jumped at the chance to tell my story about Chris and how absolutely amazing he is and was for me.

I sat next to Renea on the bus trip from the finish line down to the cemetery; I can't tell you what we spoke about because I don't remember a word of it. I remember that the whole time on that bus I was thinking about Chris and how proud I was that I'd done it. I had succeeded.

We got to the cemetery. It is immaculate; absolutely beautiful. Not a piece of grass out of place; every tombstone clean and treated with respect.

We stood there in total silence while Michelle did a reading that was impossible for me to listen to. My feet felt cemented into the ground; I couldn't move and I didn't want to move. I was with my 12 new friends, yet I felt all alone.

I was shattered, devastated and broken all at once. The reading spoke about young boys my own age, going off to war to chase an adventure but who never came home. How difficult that was to stand and listen to! All I could do was think about the great man Chris Lane. Not that Chris went off to war, but he went to the States to chase that adventure and dream of his. I stood there knowing that in 24 hours I was going back home; however, Chris didn't get that chance this time around.

We knew he came from the Western State,
Though to us he remained unknown;
For the WX was marked in his hat -
The rest a mortar had blown.

We buried him there, on the mountain spur,
where the trees are draped in moss;
We thought of his mother, no news for her

of that irreplaceable loss.

Just a boy he looked, with his snowy hair,
As we laid him down in the clay;
The padre's voice was low and clear,
No others had words to say.

Yet we knew a mother would watch and wait,
for a letter sent by her boy,
How she would dream of the things he did,
How his first words caused her joy

And as he went off to school or game,
he'd wave her fond goodbyes.
Just as he did when the great call came,
And the hot tears hurt her eyes.

Perhaps she will know in some unknown way,
Of that little rugged cross,
The remains of her hero beneath it lay,
Where the trees are draped in moss.

We cursed the foe, who stripped the dead,
No pity on them can be shown.
We marked his cross so it can be read,
"WX" Unknown.

Hearing the 7th line of the reading I became almost inconsolable, picturing in my mind the pain and anguish that I saw on the day we had to say goodbye to Chris for the final time, a moment that no family should ever have to endure and for the entire Lane family, my heart broke into 1000 pieces. I'm still in utter disbelief reading, writing and thinking about what happened to my dear friend and in turn the fact that an entire family's life has been forced to change forever.

There's no hiding or denying the fact that death is, for all of us, inevitable. I have learnt to be more accepting and open to the channels of support that are out there for me. I went through my teenage years not letting too much to get in or letting things get me down. When it did I always believed it was my problem and I would get through it alone. Chris' passing and Kokoda proved that, but that's not always the case. It's all well and good to be strong in those moments but being vulnerable and emotional is strength in itself.

I feel I owe Chris the world and was so grateful to get the chance to dedicate my trek to him. If I was to do it again, I'd dedicate it again to him. Everything I do that is of significance for the rest of my life, I'm sure I'll take Chris' legacy on board with me and bring him for the ride because I want to live the life that he wanted me to live and if he was still here I'd want him to come along for the journey with me.

People like Chris don't come along very often or maybe they do, yet they're too insecure in themselves to show that side. If I was to impart any wisdom or push anyone to do anything, it would be to show that side of yourself. I have a goal every day to make sure someone else smiles because of me; it might just be that I say a simple hello or something small. Chris helped me achieve that goal every day.

His passing has shown me not to live with any regrets, not leaving words unsaid. People will not know how you feel if you bottle it up or keep it quiet to yourself; you're no use to anyone that way. The world is full of magical brilliance and moments that you can't afford to let slip by. Every chance or opportunity is always worth taking and if you make a mistake, don't sit on it stewing about it; you've learnt something in the process of the mistake. "It is impossible to live without failing at something. Unless you live so cautiously that you might as well not have lived at all, in which case, you fail by default" (JK Rowling).

No one is perfect and no one ever will be. But by being the best, you can be like Chris was; you will be able to bring the best out in others and that in itself is perfection.

I brought a book the day I left for Kokoda, a book written by Leigh Matthews, *Accept the Challenge*. I accepted the challenge of Kokoda; I took it on, the little boy who grew into a man from Melbourne. And I won! Xxx

About the Author

Joe Pignataro is an enthusiastic man that will take any advantage to have a laugh and get the best out of every moment. It is through his vibrant nature that he excels in all that he does taking any opportunity to find the positive throughout every instance.

Nothing is too high, no challenge too difficult, no bump in the road will stop Joe from reaching his full potential. The ability to greet anyone with a smile is a constant as he will always endeavour to get the best out of others.

Joe has got a bright future ahead of him and everyone he meets along the way is a part of the journey with him

Photos in memory of fun times with my best friend Chris Lane

www.ingramcontent.com/pod-product-compliance
Lightning Source LLC
Chambersburg PA
CBHW042051290426
44110CB00001B/20